C000199135

Text: *Dennis Kelsall*
Series editor: *Tony Bowerman*
Photographs: *Dennis Kelsall, James Grant/www.
jamesgphotography, Paul Newcombe/ www.
paulnewcombephotography.co.uk, Shutterstock,
Dreamstime, Bigstock, Fotolia*

Design: *Carl Rogers*

© *Northern Eye Books Limited 2014*

*Dennis Kelsall has asserted his rights under the
Copyright, Designs and Patents Act, 1988 to be
identified as the author of this work. All rights
reserved.*

*This book contains mapping data licensed from
the Ordnance Survey with the permission of the
Controller of Her Majesty's Stationery Office.
© Crown copyright 2013. All rights reserved.
Licence number 100022856*

Northern Eye Books

ISBN 978-1-908632-06-7

*A CIP catalogue record for this book is available
from the British Library.*

www.northerneyebooks.co.uk

Cover: *Curbar Edge sunrise (Walk 8)*
Photo: *James Grant
www.jamesgphotography.co.uk*

Important Advice: The routes described in
this book are undertaken at the reader's own
risk. Walkers should take into account their
level of fitness, wear suitable footwear and
clothing, and carry food and water. It is also
advisable to take the relevant OS map with
you in case you get lost and leave the area
covered by our maps.

Whilst every care has been taken to ensure the
accuracy of the route directions, the publishers
cannot accept responsibility for errors or
omissions, or for changes in the details given.
Nor can the publisher and copyright owners
accept responsibility for any consequences
arising from the use of this book.

If you find any inaccuracies in either the text or
maps, please write or email us at the address
below. Thank you.

First published in 2014 by

Northern Eye Books Limited
*Northern Eye Books, Tattenhall, Cheshire CH3 9PX
Email: tony@northerneyebooks.com*

For sales enquiries, please call 01928 723 744

 Twitter: @Northerneyeboo
@Top10walks

Contents

Britain's First National Park

CREATED IN 1951, THE PEAK DISTRICT NATIONAL PARK extends over six counties and is the second most visited of Britain's National Parks. Its highest point lies upon the seemingly remote Kinder plateau, where a mass trespass in 1932 marked the turning point in a long and sometimes bitter campaign that led to the creation of Britain's National Parks and the open access we enjoy today.

The high, peaty moorlands of the northern Dark Peak are founded on gritstone, their stark grandeur accentuated by impressive, weather-worn tors and edges. The moors extend out of the Pennines in two horns that enclose the limestone plateau of the White Peak, an upland pasture deeply cleft by narrow gorges and dales. The transition between the two is startlingly abrupt and each has a distinctive character and beauty all its own: the wild openness of the north contrasting with a more intimate landscape dotted with small villages and crisscrossed by old lanes.

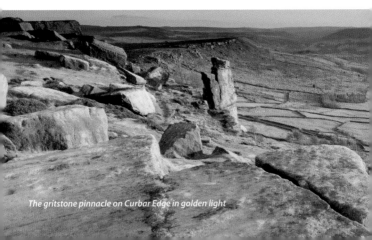

The gritstone pinnacle on Curbar Edge in golden light

Rocks and Edges

Surprisingly for newcomers, the Peak District is almost devoid of anything resembling a traditional mountain peak (the name instead derives from the Old English *paec,* merely meaning 'hill'). In reality, The Peak is a high, sloping plateau, cleft by deep valleys and winding ravines. In compensation, however, there are long runs of startlingly dramatic cliffs — here known as edges — and spectacularly weathered outcrops of rock, often referred to as tors. For rock climbers, they offer some of England's finest challenges, while for walkers the views from the escarpments' rims can be unforgettable.

"High Peak ... this, perhaps, is the most desolate, wild and abandoned country in all England."

Daniel Defoe, *A tour thro' the whole island of Great Britain,* 1724

TOP 10 **Walks:** Rocks and Edges

SEEN FROM BELOW, THE REMOTE, TOWERING and ruggedly craggy Peakland edges might appear impossibly difficult to attain. But although a handful might demand a long and sometimes strenuous walk, the majority can be reached by a moderate ramble, whose effort is handsomely rewarded by the splendid views from the top. The ten described here are amongst the most impressive and are satisfying climaxes to superb walks. Don't miss them.

Edale's Tors — page 8

Millstone Rocks — page 14

Derwent Edge — page 20

Rushup Edge — page 24

Weatherworn rocks on Kinder Edge, with Edale far below

Edale's Tors

Wild cloughs provide a passage onto the Kinder plateau for unrivalled views across the Vale of Edale

What to expect:
Rugged hill paths, sustained climb, stream crossings

Distance/time: 9km/ 5¾ miles. Allow 3 hours

Start: Edale pay and display car park

Grid ref: SK 123 853

Ordnance Survey Map: Explorer OL1 The Peak District: Dark Peak area: *Kinder Scout, Bleaklow, Black Hill & Ladybower Reservoir*

After the walk: The Old Nag's Head at Edale, S33 7ZD

Walk outline

From Edale, the walk passes through pasture and plantation into the confines of Grindsbrook Clough. Clambering out at the top, the way skirts the impressive rim of the Kinder plateau before descending steeply beside Golden Clough. The route towards the head of Grindsbrook Clough involves clambering over boulders and occasionally lies within the streambed. Although normally straightforward, it might be difficult for less experienced walkers after heavy rain or when it's icy.

The Kinder edges

The rim of the Kinder plateau runs for almost fifteen miles, enclosing nearly four square miles of featureless moorland. However, the edges are startling, littered with boulders worn by the weather into weird and wonderful forms, and falling in abrupt cliffs and ravine-like cloughs. The section here is one of the most readily accessible, but nonetheless dramatic, offering breathtaking views into the wild cloughs below and across the Vale of Edale to Mam Tor and the Great Ridge. The outward path beside Grinds Brook imparts a sense of adventure and was the original route of the Pennine Way before it was re-routed via Jacob's Ladder.

Head for the hills

Ring ouzel

The Walk

1. Leaving the car park by the toilets, turn right and walk up through the village past the **Victorian church** to the **Old Nag's Head**. Keep going as the lane degrades to a stone track to the lodge at the entrance to **Grindslow House.**

Dedicated to the Holy and Undivided Trinity, Edale's church was built in 1885 to replace an earlier chapel founded in 1633. At one time the village had no burial rights

© Crown copyright and/or database right. All rights reserved. Licence number 100022856

and the dead were carried over the hill via Hollins Cross for interment in the ancient churchyard at Hope.

2. Leave the track for a path signed on the right to 'Grinds Brook', which dips to a bridge spanning the stream. Climb steeply away and follow a flagged path left, ignoring a grass path attacking the hillside that shortly branches off by a stone hut. Through a gate, continue into a **small wood**, emerging to cross a bridge spanning the side stream of **Golden Clough**.

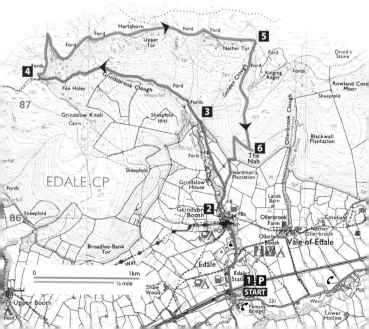

Mythical creatures: *Kinder's weatherworn boulders often resemble outlandish animals*

3. Initially, the ongoing path is broad and well-graded, but becomes increasingly rugged higher up the valley. After climbing around a bluff, the path drops back and crosses the stream. Constrained by the steep sides, there is no doubt about the route, although paths occasionally appear on both banks. Higher up, keep with the left channel as the valley splits, the way becoming more clambering. The climb culminates on a rocky slab in front of a **large cairn**.

Although the Kinder hillsides had largely been stripped of trees to create pasture before the Romans arrived, the deep, steep sided cloughs were generally left wooded as a source of firewood and timber. Without fencing, however, new growth cannot survive the incessant nibbling of sheep and few natural woodland patches remain. Where they do, native trees such as oak, birch and rowan provide cover for small birds such as the pied flycatcher and

Bold, boulder, boldest: *The curious weather worn boulders of Nether Tor*

redstart, while woodland litter harbours fungi and a wealth of invertebrates.

4. After admiring the dramatic view, turn right (north) and follow the edge above the other valley passed on the way up. Reaching the head, cross and double back above its opposite flank before turning away above the main dale.

Like the area west of Crowden Tower, the hillside is scattered with impressive weatherworn boulders, but here the edge falls away more precipitously, revealing a truly striking view across the Vale of Edale.

Containing the valley on its other side is the Great Ridge connecting Mam Tor and Lose Hill, broken by the formidable crag of Back Tor.

Eventually a **flagged path** develops, later passing a group of boulders above **Nether Tor**, one of which is pierced by a natural, vertical slit. Walk a little farther to a junction at the head of **Golden Clough**.

5. Turn right along a steeply descending flagged and stepped path, which drops below the rocky promontory of **Ringing Roger**. Joining another path lower down, it continues to a junction on a grassy knoll above **The Nab**.

6. Swing sharp right and carry on downhill, the way zigzagging to a gate at the bottom of the moor beside **Heardman's Plantation**. The onward path falls across hillside meadow to meet your outward route by the stone hut. Walk back through **Edale** to the car park, to complete the walk. ♦

The Pennine Way

Although conceived by the great champion of rambling, Tom Stephenson in 1935, the 256-mile long Pennine Way officially opened only in 1965. Meandering along the country's spine from Edale to Kirk Yetholm in the Scottish Borders, it was Britain's first National Trail. The route passes through some of England's wildest, loneliest and most evocative landscapes, alternating between intimate valleys and dales and open, desolate moors.

Winter sun spotlights the rocky slopes in Longdendale

Millstone Rocks

On a clear day, the view along the Longdendale Valley looks out across Cheshire to the distant Clwydian Range

What to expect:
Tracks and moorland paths; sustained climb onto edge

Distance/time: 9.5km/ 6 miles. Allow 3½ hours

Start/finish: Crowden car park, off A628

Grid ref: SK 072 992

Ordnance Survey Map: Explorer OL1 *The Peak District: Dark Peak area: Kinder Scout, Bleaklow, Black Hill & Ladybower Reservoir*

After the walk: The Bulls Head at Tintwistle, SK13 1JY. Snacks and drinks are available at the Camping and Caravanning Club site shop

Walk outline
Beginning near the Crowden Youth Hostel and Camping and Caravanning Club site (both excellent bases from which to explore the area), the walk joins the Pennine Way above the Torside and Rhodeswood reservoirs. Across the main road, the route zigzags up the hillside and runs through a forest fringe beneath abandoned quarries before a final easy leg across open moor to Millstone Rocks. A steady descent across the moor leads back to Crowden.

Millstone Rocks
Once part of an extensive Norman hunting forest, Longdendale is overshadowed by dark and dramatic edges on both flanks. To the south the high ground culminates in Bleaklow Hill, the Peak District's second highest summit, while to the north a vast area of almost featureless moss rises to distant Black Hill. There are several vantage points along the defining edges of the valley, and that at Millstone Rocks combines spectacular views with a superbly varied walk that savours woodland, lakeside and the open wilderness of the moor.

Leaving Highstone Rocks

Redstart

The Walk

1. Take the path from the far end of the car park to the toilets, there turning right beside the **Camping and Caravanning Club** site. At the top, go left through a gate past large farm sheds. After crossing **Crowden Brook**, the track climbs over the low shoulder of a hill, giving a foretaste of the views to be had later on. Remain with the main track, which eventually descends to meet the main road.

© Crown copyright and/or database right. All rights reserved. Licence number 100022856

2. Cross to the ongoing **Pennine Way** opposite and, ignoring the path off left into Tinsel School Wood, continue ahead through a gate into pine fringing the **Torside Reservoir**. Emerging through gates overlooking the **dam** at the far end, follow a path to the right beside a water leat. Intersecting the main service drive from the reservoir, cross diagonally left to a gated gravel track. Carry on above trees, which soon give way to reveal a view across the **Rhodeswood Reservoir**. Eventually meeting a drive rising from the **Rhodeswood Dam**, walk up to the main road.

3. Take another track diagonally opposite, which gains height onto

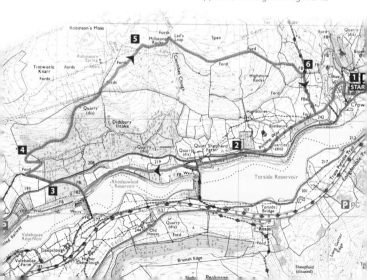

Summer sailors: *Looking across the broad expanse of Torside Reservoir*

the **moor**. Leaving the intake wall, the track winds sharply right. Where it then forks, remain with the left branch, soon climbing through another bend. Ignore a sharp right turn and continue upwards, swinging through a final bend and now heading for the top corner of a conifer plantation.

To the Normans, a royal forest was a protected hunting demesne that was not necessarily woodland, although the shelter of Longdendale would have harboured plenty of trees. Today's hillside forest is associated with the reservoirs, planted to stabilise the slopes and help purify surface water flowing into the lakes. The original conifer plantations are being replaced by broad-leaved trees to encourage diversity in the wildlife, attracting birds such as redstart, great spotted woodpecker and pied flycatchers.

4. Cross a stile beside a gate and carry on up between the trees, a delightful mixture of larch, pine and oak rising above heather, bilberry and bracken. Higher up, the trees thin to reveal a

Gate with a view: *A lone walker pauses to look out over Longdendale*

steep, bouldery hillside before the track levels beneath the gaunt cliffs of an **old quarry**. Beyond, the way narrows to a path, passing a **small waterfall** and then rising to a stile beside the gully of **Rawkins Brook** at the edge of open moorland. Take the path bearing right to cross the stream and continue initially beside it on a generally north-easterly heading towards the higher ground of **Millstone Rocks**.

The several extensive quarries in the area were worked during the 19th century and *provided stone for the construction of the railway and the reservoir dams in the valley.*

5. Finally broaching the edge of the scar, the path curves east along the rim of crags overlooking the massive scoop of **Coombes Clough**. Before long, the way turns in above a deepening gully to cross the stream of **Hollins Clough** at **Lad's Leap**. The clear path carries on past a **large cairn** and, although now set back from the edge, still offers an impressive wider view. Now gently falling, the way passes the end of a wall to continue along a shallow trough. Joining another wall, the descent

gradually steepens, shortly crossing a fence stile. The path progresses downhill to the corner of a **small plantation** and **memorial cairn**.

6. Turn through a gate on the right and follow the ongoing path at the edge of successive fields, finally to emerge onto a track. Go left and retrace your outward steps past the **campsite** to the car park, to complete the walk. ♦

Longdendale's reservoirs

Gazing out from the craggy summit of Millstone Rocks over the spectacularly rugged bowl of Coombes Clough, it is difficult to imagine the valley without the string of reservoirs that step along its length. But they were not always there. Draining a catchment of more than 30 square miles, the six reservoirs were built between 1848 and 1884 to supply water to the rapidly-growing populations of Salford and Manchester.

The Wheel Stones on Derwent Edge

Derwent Edge

A gradual climb opens up classic views across the Derwent Reservoirs, with a pleasant stroll beside the lake to finish

What to expect:
Good paths and tracks, with a steep climb to start

Distance/time: 7km/ 4¼ miles. Allow 2½ hours

Start/finish: Roadside parking on the A57 by the eastern end of the Ashopton Viaduct

Grid ref: SK 196 864

Ordnance Survey Map: Explorer OL1 The Peak District: Dark Peak area: *Kinder Scout, Bleaklow, Black Hill & Ladybower Reservoir*

After the walk: The Ladybower Inn at Bamford, S33 0AX

Walk outline

Beginning by the Ashopton Viaduct, the route winds up a track before climbing the open hillside onto Ladybower Tor. The gradient soon eases as the ridge is gained and followed over Lead Hill and Whinstone Lee Tor. The broad spine of the edge runs on to distant Back Tor, but shortly after passing the Hurkling Stones, the way drops away across the steep hillside to the Ladybower Reservoir to return by the lakeside.

Derwent Edge

The Derwent Edge runs high above the Ladybower Reservoir for nearly 5 kilometres/3 miles and is a stunning walk. While a circuit incorporating the complete ridge would involve a trek of 16 kilometres/10 miles or more, the full essence of its beauty is captured within this modest loop. The scenery is superb and there is much to contemplate, for below the dark waters are the remains of two villages, drowned when the Ladybower Dam was completed some 70 years ago. Of Ashopton, there is now no trace, but during dry summers, when the water is low, the forlorn walls of Derwent occasionally break the surface.

High House Farm estate

Curlew

The Walk

1. Walk from the roadside parking towards the **Ashopton Viaduct**, branching off right just before it up a gated service drive. Swing through the sharp right-hand bend and carry on beyond the end of the tarmac up a gravel track.

2. Keep ahead through successive gates at the top, the way signed to 'Cutthroat Bridge'. Almost immediately beyond the second gate, bear off left onto a narrow path that climbs determinedly up the bilberry and bracken-clad hillside. After swinging to the left, it ascends to a fork. Take the left branch and keep going up to reach a crossing path. Go left again, still rising but now less steeply. The path soon settles along the edge of the hill, continuing to gain height and opening a grand panorama across the valley. Before long you will come to a crossing of several paths below **Whinstone Lee Tor**. That to the left leads onto the prominence for the view.

3. The route, however, continues along the gradually rising edge. The prominent rocks ahead are the **Wheel Stones** while the more distant outcrop is **White Tor**. Keep going until you reach a junction of paths beside a cairn. Go left, the way signed to 'Derwent', descending across the heather and bracken moor. Lower down, the path is flagged, part of an ancient **packhorse causey** that took a track out of the valley and over the hills towards Sheffield. At the bottom, turn right, joining a bridleway beside a wall.

4. After a few metres, go left through a gate. The way, still signed to 'Derwent' drops to the edge of a stand of pine. Through gates, carry on alongside the trees and then pass into the National Trust's **Ashes Farm and High House Farm estate**. After fording **Grindle Clough**, wind between the restored **Grindle Barns** and follow the

© Crown copyright and/or database right. All rights reserved. Licence number 100023456

Catch light: *The last rays of the setting sun spotlight a rock on Derwent Edge*

continuing track steeply downhill to emerge onto a wide track.

Amongst the plants to be found in the wildflower meadows around the barns the delicate pale-blue harebells. Sometimes known as 'fairies thimble', they were believed to provide shelter for fairies, but more sinisterly were also associated with witches, who supposedly used the plant as an ingredient in their flying potions.

5. To the left the track meanders above the lakeshore through grazing and then woodland. It ends through a gate onto the service track at **Ashopton**. Fork right and walk back down to the road to complete the walk. ♦

Woodlands for wildlife

Forests are widely planted above reservoirs to stabilise the banks, filter runoff water and provide a cash crop. During the early 20th century, quick-growing Sitka spruce was often chosen, but little wildlife can survive such a dense monoculture. More recent plantings include native Scots pine, birch and oak that encourage a diversity of mammals, birds and insects, and the bright woodland flowers of the understorey.

Cloud shadows dapple the ridge-top path along Rushup Edge

Rushup Edge

*An unassuming walk onto a narrowing ridge that brings
surprisingly dramatic views at its eastern end*

What to expect:
*Good paths; a long but
steady climb*

Distance/time: 8.5km/ 5½ miles. Allow 3 hours

Start: Barber Booth car park

Grid ref: SK 107 847

Ordnance Survey Map: Explorer OL1 The Peak District: Dark Peak
area: *Kinder Scout, Bleaklow, Black Hill & Ladybower Reservoir*

After the walk: The Old Nag's Head at Edale, S33 7ZD

Walk outline

*After briefly backtracking along the lane, the route strikes across
valley grazing past Manor House Farm to Chapel Gate. It is then a
settled plod up the hill to the top of the ridge. The walk progresses
along the ridge, which narrows beyond the summit. Abandoning
the ridge at Mam Nick, the route drops steeply from the northern
flank of Mam Tor to Greenlands, returning easily across the fields to
Barber Booth.*

Rushup Edge

Rushup Edge is the western extension of the Great Ridge and,
although its top, Lord's Seat is higher than Mam Tor, walkers
often ignore it in preference to the more popular section
over Mam Tor and Back Tor to Lose Hill. Beginning simply as a
broad saddle, Lord's Seat gradually asserts a separate identity
from the high ground enclosing the head of the Vale of Edale.
Narrowing dramatically beyond the summit, steep, grassy
slopes fall on either side, and a spectacular panorama opens
into three separate valleys. However, it is the view ahead that is
particularly eye-catching as the ground drops to the high pass
of Mam Nick and the long ridge beyond.

Returning to Barber Booth

Meadow pipit

The Walk

1. Head back down the lane from the **Barber Booth car park**. Some 100 metres after passing beneath the railway viaduct, leave over a stile beside a gate on the right to a track. Beyond a stile diagonally opposite, bear left to the far corner of the field by a range of roofless farm buildings. A path runs alongside them, shortly slipping over a stile to carry on at the edge of a pasture. Leave through a gate in the corner and strike a diagonal course across a couple of rough fields to a stile next to a gate in the top wall.

2. Now on a track, **Chapel Gate**, go right through a gate and continue

steadily upwards across the hillside for some 1.6 kilometres/1 mile.

For most people, a gate is simply something to pass through, but in this part of the world, the word can also mean a track. Many have their origins in the ancient packhorse trails that criss-crossed the hills to connect the various valleys and settlements and served as the motorways of their day. Cut Gate near Margery Hill and Doctor's Gate on Shelf Moor are other examples in the area.

The increasing height expands the view across the head of the Vale of Edale, a great basin that captures the headwaters of the River Noe. Far below, the railway enters a deep cutting at the mouth of the

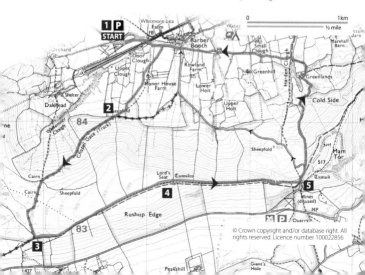

© Crown copyright and/or database right. All rights reserved. Licence number 100022856

Edge of heaven: *A wind-sculpted tree echoes the angles along the ridge*

Cowburn Tunnel, which takes the line out of the Peak towards Manchester. It was constructed in 1891, navvies burrowing in from each end and outwards from a central shaft sunk from the top of the hill. At one point, incoming spring water flooded the shaft to a depth of 90 metres and, until it could be drained, work continued within a diving bell.

Keep with the main track, which eventually levels at the crest of the hill, shortly reaching a junction.

3. The way is to the left, climbing gently beside a stone wall. At first, the wider views are obscured. However, farther on, Eldon Hill appears to the right, its flank eaten away by a massive limestone quarry that was worked for 50 years until 1999. Across the Vale of Edale to the north is the Kinder plateau. Carry on to the top of **Lord's Seat**.

Marking the summit of Lord's Seat is the mound of a Bronze Age burial cairn or tumulus, erected some 3,000 years or more ago for the burial of a local chieftain. It is one of several dotting the surrounding hills,

Breezy ridge: *A party of walkers heading along Rushup Edge from Lord's Seat*

---

including Mam Tor, on which there was a sizeable defended settlement.

4. Continue along the ridge beyond the highpoint.

The view suddenly opens ahead along the Great Ridge, a term coined by the late W. A. Poucher, whose splendid mountain photographs inspired a generation.

The path sticks by the narrowing crest and finally drops sharply to the lane at **Mam Nick**.

5. Walk down to the left, crossing to leave through a gate by the bus stop. Where the path then forks, take the left branch, which drops quite steeply straight down the hill. Eventually coming off the moor, the way winds between hawthorn and gorse to end through a couple of gates onto a metalled track at **Greenlands**.

6. Carry on down the hill, the way signed to 'Edale'. After passing through a fern-banked cutting, the track winds across a stream in **Harden Clough**. Immediately, look for a stile up on the left. Head out across the fields, eventually descending steps to cross a

stream in a small gully. Farther on the path drops into a deep wooded clough to cross another stream. Now on a contained path, walk on to cross a final stream and continue over two more fields to emerge onto the lane beside a bridge across the **River Noe**. Take the narrow lane opposite, which meanders up beneath the **railway viaduct** back to the car park, to complete the walk. ♦

Cotton grass

Although it looks like grass, cotton grass is actually a sedge and thrives across the wet, mossy uplands of the Pennines. For most of the year, it is hardly distinguishable amongst the tussock, but in early summer, its tiny flowers produce fluffy white cottonwool-like balls that dance in the breeze. While the soft, downy hairs are unsuitable for spinning, they were once collected as stuffing for pillows and mattresses.

Looking down on Ladybower Reservoir from Bamford Edge

Bamford Edge

Overlooking the Derwent Valley, this dramatic edge offers unsurpassed views over Ladybower Reservoir

What to expect:
Good moorland paths, an initial steep climb along a track from the village

Distance/time: 5km/ 3 miles. Allow 2 hours

Start: Bamford, roadside parking in the village

Grid ref: SK 207 835

Ordnance Survey Map: Explorer OL1 The Peak District: Dark Peak area: *Kinder Scout, Bleaklow, Black Hill & Ladybower Reservoir*

After the walk: Anglers Rest, Bamford, S33 0DY

Walk outline

Leaving the main road at Bamford, the route climbs steeply from the valley along an old track. Crossing the lane at the top, it continues more easily over open moor to an old quarry. Skirting that, the way soon joins the edge, following it to an impressive viewpoint overlooking the valley. The return slants back across a bracken hillside before reversing the steep track to the village.

Bamford

Named after an ancient bridge and ford across the Derwent, Bamford grew with the founding of the Hope-Pennistone turnpike around 1770. At the beginning of the 19th century, a new cotton spinning mill beside the river brought further expansion, its benevolent owners, the Moores, supporting the construction of a church, school and workers' housing in the village. Subsequently converted to steam, the mill operated until 1967 when its buildings were converted into apartments. The construction of the Derwent dams in the 20th century brought even more people, but the flooding of Ashopton and Derwent Bridge villages left Bamford as the highest village in the valley.

Entering Bamford Moor

Lapwing

The Walk

1. Begin from the small triangular tree-sheltered 'green' beside the main road in the centre of the village, climbing away along **Fiddlers Well**. Reaching a junction, keep ahead up **Bamford Clough**, a narrow lane marked 'unsuitable for motor vehicles'. Bear right at a fork in front of the entrance to **Clough House**, the way deteriorating to a rough track that climbs steeply within a belt of trees.

Higher up, the trees thin, first to the right and then to the left, opening views down to the Hope Valley and then across the vale of the Derwent to the distinctive summit of Win Hill. *Ahead to the left on the skyline are the rugged crags of Bamford Edge.*

2. Meeting a **narrow lane** at the top, go right, walking to the crest of the hill where there is a gate and stile on the left. Leave the lane for the **open access land** and take the clear path slanting off to the right, which gains height easily through a sea of tall bracken. *There are views across to Stanage Edge and Burbage Rocks above Hathersage and back across the Hope Valley to Shatton Edge and Offerton Moor.*

Ignoring crossing sheep tracks, climb ahead, shortly passing between high heather-covered mounds, the spoil from an **abandoned quarry** that lies a few metres farther on. *The quarry provided stone for the construction of the mill and other buildings down in the village.*

© Crown copyright and/or database right. All rights reserved. Licence number 100022856

Rain on the wind: *Win Hill and Ladybower Reservoir seen from rocks on Bamford Edge*

At the entrance to the quarry, the path rises to the right, skirting around its rim to a junction of paths at the northern tip.

3. Keep going on the more pronounced middle path, which soon joins with another path rising from the left. The way continues ahead along the edge of a developing low escarpment.

4. Reaching the high point, take a sheep path off to the left, which leads across a terrace of ling heather to a prominent **outcrop of rocks**. Now on the edge proper, follow the run of high cliffs that carries on to the north west for another 500 metres. The edge culminates in **Great Tor**, where a spectacular view suddenly opens ahead to the Ladybower Dam and Ashopton Viaduct.

The high, overhanging slabs of the cliffs here are a favourite of experienced rock climbers, but mere walkers will be content to admire the superb views. Across the valley, beyond Win Hill, is Lose Hill and Mam Tor, with the higher ground of the

Final seconds: *The last rays of the sun catch the hills above Ladybower Reservoir*

Kinder plateau rising behind. To the north, overlooking the long arm of the reservoir is Derwent Edge, which rises beyond Dovestone Tor to the high point of Back Tor.

5. Although the path continues beyond a crossing wall, the escarpment runs out here and it is time to turn back.

There are around twenty stone circles scattered across the Peak District. One of the smallest lies about 0.5 kilometre to the east of the ridge, overlooking the catchment of Hood Brook. Occupying

a small terrace set into the gentle slope of the hill, six stones form a rough circle within a low earth bank some 10 metres in diameter. It dates from the late Neolithic or Early Bronze Age and is perhaps some 3,500 years old. The circle is part of a much wider pattern of burial cairns, field systems and other sites that point to the moors being relatively well-settled at that time.

Retrace your steps along the edge of the high cliffs. However, when you reach the point where you first joined them, instead of going left, keep straight ahead. Remain with the more prominent path, which gently loses height across the bracken-clad hillside. Watch for it

shortly curving right and then left to join with a lower path, which runs on across the slope of the hill back to the stile and gate at which you left the lane on the way up (**2**).

Turn right and retrace your outward route down **Bamford Clough** to return to the village and complete the walk. ♦

The Derwent reservoirs

Ladybower was the last of the three Derwent Valley reservoirs to be built, its opening delayed by the Second World War. The construction brought an influx of labourers who were housed at Birchinlee, a temporary village of corrugated iron buildings known locally as 'Tin Town'. A supply railway ran from the main line at Bamford Station up the Derwent Valley to Howden, transporting stone from the quarries at Bole Hill.

An abandoned millstone below Stanage Edge

Stanage Edge

A pleasant wander along the most popular edge in the Peak District

What to expect:
paths are uneven in Whitfield Gill, one lengthy ascent

Distance/time: 8km/ 5 miles. Allow 2½ hours

Start/finish: Upper Burbage Bridge car park, beside A625

Grid ref: SK 259 829

Ordnance Survey Map: Explorer OL1 The Peak District: Dark Peak area: *Kinder Scout, Bleaklow, Black Hill & Ladybower Reservoir*

After the walk: The Norfolk Arms, Ringinglow, S11 7TS

Walk outline

Striking across the moss, the route bypasses the Cowper Stone to gain the eastern end of Stanage Edge. An easy path traces the rim of the escarpment, passing above a rocky aerie known locally as Robin Hood's Cave. Farther on, an old packhorse track offers a detour to Stanedge Pole on its low hill in the middle of the moor. Returning to the edge, the way drops back through Stanage Plantation and on across the hillside footing the cliffs. The final leg climbs back onto the edge and reverses the outward path to the car park at Upper Burbage Bridge.

Stanage Edge

Running for some 5.5 kilometres/3½ miles, Stanage is the longest of the Peak's eastern gritstone edges and defines an abrupt boundary to the Hallam Moors on the outskirts of Sheffield. Once part of a private grouse shoot, it was forbidden land to walkers and climbers, who nevertheless braved the gamekeepers for the stolen pleasures of its rocky challenges and superlative views. Today the area is designated 'open access' and is justifiably popular.

Gritstone climber

Stonechat

The Walk

1. From the car park, follow the lane west from the bridge, leaving ahead on the bend along a broad path across the moss. Approaching the escarpment, the prominent detached rock seen over to the right is the **Cowper Stone**, which, despite its size, offers several difficult challenges to rock climbers. Picking an easy passage between the rocks, the path rises onto the escarpment and leads past a 'trig' column perched upon a cantilevered slab of rock.

© Crown copyright and/or database right. All rights reserved. Licence number 100022856

There is a fine view along the length of the edge, while equally eye-catching in the other direction is the vista beyond Hathersage along the Derwent Valley. Looking west of north across the unbroken expanse of White Path Moss, keen eyes will spot Stanedge Pole, while a glimpse to the foot of the cliff below the 'trig' will reveal a group of abandoned millstones. These can be conveniently visited on the way back.

2. Carry on along the rim of the edge. After 800 metres/½ mile watch for a path branching left through a shallow gully (SK 244 835), which leads to a narrow terrace fronting **Robin Hood's Cave**.

Agile explorers will be able to scramble through the cave to emerge onto a balcony that gives a superb view across the valley, but take care near the edge as there is a precipitous drop.

3. Having taken in the view, climb back to the top path and

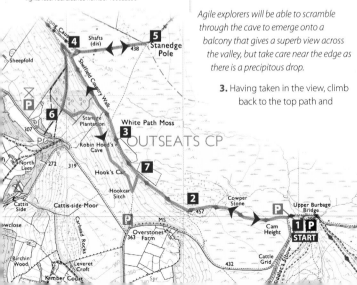

Autumn afternoon: *Alternate sunlight and short showers enliven Stanage Edge*

continue along the edge, shortly joining a broken wall above a dramatic section of cliff. Walk on some 800 metres/½ mile, crossing a ranch stile to reach a junction of paths.

4. Go right to a broad track, the **Long Causey** and follow it right for 400 metres/¼ mile to the **Stanedge Pole**.

The tall wooden post is a medieval guide stoop, which stands on the watershed of the moss from which there is a view down to the Redmires Reservoirs, the Rivelin Valley and Sheffield.

5. Retrace your steps to the top of the cliffs and follow the path right for 100 metres. At a fork, branch left, the path almost immediately doubling back to descend below the line of cliffs towards the top corner of the **Stanage Plantation**. Through a gate, follow the path into the trees. Cross a sparkling **spring** dashing from the rocks above and continue between the rowan, alder, birch and oak to emerge through a gate at the bottom.

Edge to edge?: *Panoramic views from*
Stanage Edge towards Millstone Edge

6. Ignore the obvious onward path
dropping towards the lane and instead
go left on a faint trod rising beside the
fence. It shortly joins a broader path
that leads to a gap in a wall on the
right. Breaking from the trees, carry on
across the hillside, where the expanse
of deep bracken is broken in summer
by occasional tall spikes of foxglove.
Criss-crossing sheep tracks and climbers'
paths can be confusing, but keep
generally ahead with the more obvious
path, contouring the slope, remaining
parallel to the line of cliffs above.

Eventually, the path forks prominently
beside a **large boulde**r in which a
basin has been hollowed from its top.
Take the right branch, which angles
down towards a roadside car park by
a junction. However, shortly reaching
another obvious junction of paths, turn
left and climb towards the cliffs. The
path winds easily between the boulders
onto the top of the edge.

7. Turn right towards the **OS 'trig' point**,
which lies about 500 metres away. As
you approach the 'trig', look for a path
branching down between the rocks to
the base of the cliffs. *There you will find*
the group of millstones seen earlier in the

day. They were abandoned when white bread became fashionable and the market collapsed in the mid-18th century.

Return to the top of the cliffs and retrace your outward track past the 'trig' point and back to the car park at **Upper Burbage Bridge** to complete the walk. ♦

Stanedge Pole

The track to Stanedge Pole follows the course of a Roman road that linked the forts at Templeborough and Navio. The same route was subsequently followed by packhorse teams and known as the Long Causey, the tall pole being erected as a conspicuous marker on this otherwise featureless landscape. Although the wooden pole is periodically renewed, dates carved on its rocky base stretch back to 1550.

On top of the aptly named Millstone Edge

Millstone Edge

This walk has it all: old quarries, dramatic edges striking tors, and a babbling stream in a delightful wooded valley

What to expect:
Woodland and moorland paths

Distance/time: 7km/ 4½ miles. Allow 2 hours

Start: Longshaw Lodge National Trust pay and display car park

Grid ref: SK 266 800

Ordnance Survey Map: Explorer OL1 The Peak District: Dark Peak area: *Kinder Scout, Bleaklow, Black Hill & Ladybower Reservoir*

After the walk: Tearoom at Longshaw Lodge (National Trust); or The Grouse, beside the A625 at Nether Padley, S11 7TZ

Walk outline

Winding through the Longshaw Estate, the route descends into the ancient oak woodland of Padley Gorge. The way continues beneath the Bolehill quarries, crossing the main road to rise along Millstone Edge onto Over Owler Tor. The way back lies through the rocks to the road by Owler Tor and then rejoins Burbage Brook. After heading upstream, the ramble finally returns through the woodland of the Longshaw Estate to the Lodge.

Millstone Edge

The outcropping millstone grit above Padley has long been quarried, the stone used for the construction of the Derwent Valley dams and, of course, millstones, many of which can be found abandoned amongst the workings. Now the haunt of rock climbers, the quarry faces are hardly recognisable for what they once were, but the extensive flat aprons beneath the cliffs unmistakably identify working floors. Hidden in the woodland colonising the base of the quarry cliffs is a causeway. It led to an incline down which blocks of stone were lowered to the railway for transport to the Howden and Derwent dams.

Mother Cap

Fox in the rocks

The Walk

1. Take the path from the car park towards the **visitor centre**. Just before reaching it, turn right at a junction to the main drive. Cross to a footpath opposite, which drops left to run below **Longshaw Lodge**. Entering a clump of trees, keep right to continue beside rhododendrons above a **ha ha**.

Pronounced as an expression of mirth rather than a eureka moment, the ditches were a way of preventing grazing livestock encroaching from the outer park into the more formal garden areas without detracting from the view.

Passing through gates, walk on beside grazing and then between more rhododendrons into open woodland. Stick with the main path around the perimeter of a **small lake** and on at the edge of the wood. Where the path then forks, keep ahead, passing a restored barn that now serves as an **information centre**, to come out onto the B6521. Cross to the

footpath opposite and descend right to a footbridge over **Burbage Brook**.

2. Follow the waterside path downstream, the way signed 'Padley Gorge'. Passing into oak and birch woodland, the path heads into the **deepening gorge** high above the stream, where the hillside is littered with moss-covered boulders.

3. After 800 metres, at a fork, bear off right towards 'Surprise View' and 'Bole Hill Quarry'. Where a quarry track shortly drops from the right, keep ahead and pass through a broken wall. Curve right to a gate and continue through a second gate into open birch wood.

© Crown copyright and/or database right. All rights reserved. Licence number 100022856

Catchlight: *The first rays of the sun illuminate rocks near Over Owler Tor*

Where the path forks, branch left past **old quarry workings** to a second fork. Now swing right up a short stony path onto the top of the cliff and cross an open space into more birch wood. Although muted by the trees, the quarry area remains readily discernible. The working face lies over to the right, while to the left is the embankment of a tramway. Keep a lookout too for an abandoned stone trough, which lies to the right of the path.

Soon after passing the trough and as the cliffs run out, watch for a fork. Take the right, less distinct branch, which winds onto the higher ground. Scale a stile beside a gate and go left through another gate to the road.

4. Cross to a path opposite, and walk left past a viewpoint overlooking the **Derwent Valley**. Pick up a gravel path to a gate onto access land. Leaving the gravel, follow the fence left along the edge. Occasional stiles lead to viewpoints on top of the cliffs, but the route remains on this side of the fence.

Strange stone: *Mothercap dominates the path between Over Owler Tor and Owler Tor*

After 600 metres, the fence curves right. Passing a stile, branch right at an obvious fork and head towards the rocks of **Over Owler Tor**. Gaining the ridge, wander left to the highpoint for the view.

5. Briefly retrace your steps to take a gently descending path towards the prominent outcrop of **Mother Cap**. Pick your way onwards through the boulders, many of which require little imagination to envisage bizarre creatures; look out for a toad and the head of Nessie, while nearby is an **unfinished millstone**. Walk

on into birch wood, but towards the far side, as a car park becomes visible, watch for a fork. Bear left and walk out to a gate beside the main road.

6. Cross and drop to a kissing-gate. To the right is the outcrop of **Owler Tor**, but the onward way lies to the left, the path descending an old track through a heathery gully. Ignore a right fork and continue to the footbridge at the top of **Padley Gorge**. Now back at (**2**), remain on this bank and follow a path upstream beside the brook to a second bridge. *Keep an eye open for dippers and occasional grey wagtails bobbing amongst the rocks.*

7. Over the bridge, follow a path up to a cascading stream. At a junction just beyond, go right to re-cross the stream and carry on through mixed wood. After passing through a gate, eventually emerge onto the road. Cross to a drive onto the **Longshaw estate**. Approaching the visitor centre and tearoom, turn left and left again back to the car park to complete the walk. ♦

Longshaw Lodge

Longshaw Lodge was built for the 5th Duke of Rutland in 1827 to host moorland grouse shoots and scenic woodland rides. During the Great War, the lodge became a convalescent home for soldiers wounded in France. Later bought by Sheffield Corporation, the estate opened to the public and then passed to the National Trust. The lodge was used as a holiday home before being converted into residences.

The last rays of the sun illuminate Curbar Edge

Baslow & Curbar Edges

Two dramatic edges for the price of one, with views across the Derwent Valley, starting from a pretty, riverside pub

What to expect:
*A steady initial climb;
some quiet lanes*

Distance/time: 9km/ 5½ miles. Allow 3 hours

Start/finish: The old bridge, Calver (roadside parking)

Grid ref: SK 247 744

Ordnance Survey Map: Explorer OL24 Peak District: White Peak area: *Buxton, Bakewell, Matlock & Dovedale*

After the walk: The Bridge Inn, Calver S32 3XA

Walk outline

An initial climb from the Derwent leads to Curbar, where the way continues through fields onto a heathy terrace below Baslow Edge. Gaining the cliffs at their southern end, there is a detour to the Wellington Monument and Eagle Stone before a superb 2.5 kilometre/1½ mile ramble along the edge. The return is through the semi-natural woodland and old fields that apron the base of the cliffs, eventually dropping back through Curbar to the river.

The Edges

Baslow and Curbar Edges are part of a long and fragmented moorland escarpment. They overlook the eastern bank of the River Derwent throughout its course within the National Park, from its source on Howden Moor. Readily accessible, both edges are popular local beauty spots and favourites with rock climbers who come to practise on the high, weather-worn cliffs. As well as the grand panoramic views across the valley to the west, the outcrops provide endless subjects for imaginative minds in envisaging strange creatures amongst the boulders, while the heath and the woodland below are rich in wild flowers.

Eagle Stone

Heather and dew

The Walk

1. Begin opposite **The Bridge Inn,** walking beside the church up **Curbar Hill**.

2. Reaching a junction beside a red telephone box, turn right into **Cliff Lane**. After 200 metres, just past the white gates of **Curbar Croft**, clamber over a stile on the left and follow a contained path signed 'Baslow via Gorsbank Farm'. Over another stile, go left and then shortly bear right at a fork, before long emerging onto a drive at the entrance to **Lane Farm**.

3. Crossing, follow a short intake to a gate and stile. As you then carry on across a hay meadow, look left to see the **Round House**. Beyond a stile in the corner, veer right to join a path contouring the hillside of heath, open wood, hawthorn scrub and moss-covered boulders.

A few metres along, five rough stones lie in a grass hollow on the right. They bear only initials and mark the graves of the Cundy family, who lived at Grislowfield Farm, lower down the hill. The family was hit by an outbreak of plague that spread through the village in 1632, 32 years before it struck nearby Eyam.

After crossing a wall, branch left at a fork, the path now angling upwards. Reaching a diamond crossing, keep ahead, the way signed as a bridleway to 'Blackstone Edge'. Rising to the corner of a wall, carry on above it. Keep left at a fork, following the

© Crown copyright and/ or database right. All rights reserved. Licence number 100022856

Evening light: *A horizontal sun throws long shadows across Curbar Edge*

main path round to join another track. Carry on up the hill.

4. Reaching a fork at the top of the rise, bear right on a short detour to the **Wellington Monument**, which lies just a few metres farther on. *It was erected in 1866 by Colonel E M Wrench, an army doctor who had served in the Crimea, to commemorate the Iron Duke.*

There turn left across the moor to another local curiosity, a prominent outcrop known as the **Eagle Stone**, perhaps a corruption of *Aegle* — an ancient goddess of health.

Go left back to point (**4**) and there turn off right along a rough path that follows the rim of **Baslow Edge**. *Towards the far end of the run of cliffs, an etched plaque beside a viewing platform identifies landmarks along the skyline.* An easy access path leads out to the lane.

5. Cross to the ongoing path opposite, climbing through a kissing-gate. Fork left off the main path to pick up an informal path along the top of the edge.

Misty magic: *A lambent first light licks the rocks along Curbar Edge*

The rock here was quarried for millstones; one can be seen in the rubble below the cliffs, while another lies a little farther along beside the path. Eventually the path gradually loses height and drops past a clump of birch trees.

6. Immediately beyond the trees, look for a waypost and double back left onto a path that drops from the clifftop. After an initial steep descent between the rocks, the way settles easily through woodland beneath the cliffs. In time the trees thin to reveal crumbling stone walls defining abandoned fields that

have succumbed to bracken. The trail ultimately passes out through a gate near a cottage onto the sharp bend of a lane.

7. Go down the hill, leaving after 100 metres through a small gate on the right. Strike out across a small paddock to the remnants of a stile in the corner and carry on down the hill, weaving between a pair of venerable sycamores. Ignore the path shortly signed off through a gate to 'Froggatt' and instead pass through the wicket gate just beyond to continue on the other flank of the wall. Walk through a small recreation field, leaving at the

bottom corner along a track onto a back lane in the village. Turn left but then, in front of a white-doored barn, bear right. Wind between cottages and, at the next junction, go right again to the main lane.

8. Turn right, continuing straight down the hill past the red telephone box (**2**) to return to the **Bridge Inn** and complete the walk. ♦

Curbar's Round House

Although square in plan with just two tiny rooms set one above the other, Curbar's Round House is capped with a curious conical stone roof. Built around 1780, it perhaps served as a lockup, although tales suggest it may alternatively have been a 'pest house' for the confinement of infectious people, or even a bathhouse. Today, however, it's a private home.

The striking Nelson's Monument on Birchen Edge

Birchen & Gardom's Edges

Monuments to two of Britain's historic military leaders overlook the Derwent Valley above Baslow

What to expect:
Moorland tracks and paths; a short, steep ascent

Distance/time: 7km/ 4½ miles. Allow 2½ hours

Start/finish: Car park next to the Robin Hood Inn, beside A619 east of Baslow

Grid ref: SK 280 721

Ordnance Survey Map: Explorer OL24 Peak District: White Peak area: *Buxton, Bakewell, Matlock & Dovedale*

After the walk: The Robin Hood Inn at Baslow, DE45 1PQ

Walk outline

The walk begins with a short pull onto Birchen Edge. After following the cliffs past the Nelson Monument to the highpoint, the route falls across heathland to the road. Crossing to pick up an ancient packhorse trail to the Wellington Monument, the way then drops through oak woods to Bar Brook and the road. The return climbs below Gardom's Edge before a final descent across open heath.

Ancient Edges

Gardom's Edge immortalises the name of a prominent local textile family who, with John Pares in 1778, founded the cotton mill that stands by the bridge at Calver. 'Birchen' perhaps refers to the swathes of birch growing at its foot, a remnant of the woodland that would once have spread across the moors. Additional to the 19th-century monuments passed on the walk, the area is rich in relics that demonstrate a flourishing prehistoric agriculture. Archaeology has identified a wealth of field boundaries, hut circles and burial cairns and even a remarkable boulder carved with Bronze Age cup and ring marks.

Ancient 'waypost'

Bilberries

The Walk

1. From the car park, head up the hill away from the pub. After 200 metres, bear off left beside the drive of a house to a gate and stile into trees. A path climbs away at the edge of the wood, shortly levelling to reach a fork. Go right on a stepped path that clambers in a direct assault on the hillside.

2. At the top, the path meanders left along the rim of the cliffs towards the slender column of the **Nelson's Monument**, which shortly comes into view.

The three massive boulders nearby are carved with the names of naval warships that saw service at Trafalgar: Victory — Nelson's flagship, Royal Soverin (sic) — Collingwood's flagship, and Defiance — claimed to be the fastest 74-gun ship of the fleet.

Continue past the monument as the cliffs then fall away to reach the 'trig' point, some 150 metres farther on.

3. There the path forks. Take the left branch, which drops to birch-covered heath. Meeting a crossing path, go right. The heath soon gives way to moss, which can be wet in places. Occasional duckboards carry the path, which descends gently to leave the moor beside a junction.

4. Cross to the lane opposite, which is signed to 'Curbar'. After some 200 metres, leave

© Crown copyright and/or database right. All rights reserved. Licence number 100022856

Winter light: *Weathered gritstone boulders and wiry moor grasses on Gardom's Edge*

through a gate on the left to follow a restricted byway, an **old packhorse route**. A little way along to the left are **two standing stones**. *One is a poetic work of modern art while the other is an ancient waypost, erected to guide travellers across this open and often bleak landscape. Notice the archaic spelling and spacing of the letters, a technique often employed by masons cutting gravestones who, irrespective of word endings, simply started a new line as space ran out.*

Before long the path passes the **Wellington Monument**, a massive cross fashioned from millstone grit blocks.

Over to the right is an isolated outcrop called the **Eagle Stone**. *Traditionally, young men of the area proved their worthiness for marriage by climbing onto its top, not necessarily an easy feat and a challenge still taken by today's climbers.*

Continue beyond the monument along the track to a junction and bear left, heading downhill to a gate.

5. Instead of passing through, turn sharp left on a path that descends

'I saw three ships': *These rocks on Birchen Edge are named after Trafalgar warships*

gently beside a wall at the foot of a bracken and boulder-clad heath. It soon passes into a thick wood of twisted oak. Reaching the corner of the wall, swing right, now dropping more steeply through the trees. At the bottom of the wood, follow a contained path that skirts the garden of a house down to a narrow **packhorse bridge**. Over it, carry on to emerge onto the main road.

6. Cross to a stile beside a **stone drinking trough** opposite, positioned to refresh teams of horses dragging loaded carts up the long hill. Walk on to a second stile and continue behind a cottage across the hillside below a wood, where the steadily increasing height opens a view across **Derwent Valley**. Crossing the corner of a broken wall, keep ahead, eventually leaving the trees to pass between the uprights of an old gateway. The path now gradually loses height across heath and open grazing, ultimately leaving at the bottom corner onto the main road. Go left and left again to return to the car park and complete the walk.

Robin Hood might traditionally be associated with Nottingham, but legends

of his deeds are to be found throughout the Peak District and beyond. The prodigious flight of one of his arrows is said to have cut a nick into Robin Hood's Picking Rods, the shafts of a pair of Saxon crosses below Cown Edge near Glossop and Little John's grave can be found in St Michael's churchyard at Hathersage. Robin Hood himself is said to be buried at Kirklees Priory near Brighouse. ♦

Commemorative monuments

The slender Nelson's Monument was erected five years after his death by John Brightman, who also carved the names of ships in Nelson's fleet at Trafalgar on the three outcrops nearby. Across the valley, Wellington's memorial by Dr Lieutenant Colonel E. M. Wrench appeared in 1866, perhaps to ensure that the army was not outshone by the navy or maybe to remember Wellington's visit to the Duke of Rutland's nearby estate.

The Roaches' rugged gritstone has long been a favourite with climbers

The Roaches

Although not the highest point in Staffordshire, there are clear-day views right across Cheshire to North Wales

What to expect:
A stiff climb at the start onto an undulating path that extends the full length of the ridge

Distance/time: 6.5km/ 4 miles. Allow 2½ hours

Start/finish: Minor lane north of Upper Hulme

Grid ref: SK 004 621

Ordnance Survey Map: Explorer OL24 Peak District: White Peak area: *Buxton, Bakewell, Matlock & Dovedale*

After the walk: Roaches Tearoom at Upper Hulme, ST13 8TY

Walk outline

The initial climb is relieved by a short stretch through the thick pinewood footing the cliffs. After a final pull onto the top there is a spectacular but easy ramble along the edge of The Roaches to the summit 'trig' point. Beyond, the path falls gently to Roach End from which you can return, either by the outward route above the cliffs or along the lane beneath the lower outcrop of Five Clouds.

The Roaches

The Roaches are the most impressive of the Peak's western edges, part of a four-mile gritstone ridge overlooking the Staffordshire countryside. It has long been popular with rock climbers and many of the sport's top names have developed their craft on the outcropping cliffs. Rockhall, the tiny cottage beneath the cliffs was extended in 1862 from an original cave dwelling to house a gamekeeper for the Swythamley estate. In the 1970s it became home to Doug Moller, self-styled 'King of the Roaches', but was subsequently bought by the British Mountaineering Council as a climbing hut and dedicated to the memory of Don Whillans, one of England's climbing heroes.

Roaches climber

Little owl

The Walk

1. Leave the lane through a gate by the bus lay-by, from which a broad track rises away across the moor towards the broad col separating **The Roaches** and

© Crown copyright and/or database right. All rights reserved. Licence number 100022856

Hen Cloud, the neighbouring outcrop to the right. Take the path branching off left a short way up, which leads to **Rockhall Cottage**. Bear left again in front of the entrance, following a stone wall to a gap. Turn into the pinewood and follow a winding path between the boulders and trees. Before long, the way swings right to become a stepped path that clambers through a breech in the rocks onto the top of the cliff.

2. A clear path runs away to the left, shortly passing a small, dark tarn, **Doxey Pool**. *Legend says that it is inhabited by Jenny Greenteeth, a malevolent spirit who attempts to lure passers-by to a watery grave.*

However, ominous airs are quickly dispelled by the spectacular view as the path meanders easily along the edge to the trig column occupying its high point.

3. Beyond the summit, the path descends along the heathy ridge. After passing the weatherworn outcrop of **Bearstone Rock**, it finally drops to the lane at **Roach End**, where an ice-cream van often parks at weekends. If you wish, having gained

Sublime country: *The distinctive Staffordshire moors seen from the Roaches*

the height, you can continue along the ridge for another 2.5 kilometres/1½ miles to the final outcrop, **Hanging Stone**. In fine weather, it is a lovely walk.

4. It is a pleasant stroll back to the parking area along the quiet lane to the left, or alternatively, retrace your outward steps along the ridge. By way of variation, you can then continue past the point at which you broached the cliff (**2**). A path descends the left flank of the ridge to the moor, curving right beyond the rocks to meet the path running over the col. Turn right, back to the lane to complete the walk. ♦

Wild wallabies

During the 1930s, Captain Brocklehurst of Roaches Hall maintained a private zoo on his estate, which included llamas, emus, and wallabies. It closed at the start of the Second World War, but some wallabies escaped into the wild. For many years they were a common, if unusual, sight amidst the hills, reputedly wandering as far as Kinder. More recently, numbers have declined and the group is thought to have all but died out.

Useful Information

Visit Peak District & Derbyshire
The Peak's official tourism website covers everything from accommodation and special events to attractions and adventure. **www.visitpeakdistrict.com**

Peak District National Park
The Peak District National Park website also has information on things to see and do, plus a host of practical details to help plan your visit. **www.peakdistrict.org**

Tourist Information Centres
The main TICs provide free information on everything from accommodation and transport to what's on and walking advice..

Bakewell	01629 816558	bakewell@peakdistrict.gov.uk
Castleton	01629 816572	castleton@peakdistrict.gov.uk
Moorland Centre	01433 670207	edale@peakdistrict.gov.uk
Upper Derwent	01433 650953	derwentinfo@peakdistrict.gov.uk

Rail Travel
Four railway service cross the National Park:

The Hope Valley Line

The Derwent Valley Line

The Manchester to Buxton Line

The Manchester to Glossop Line

Information from National Rail Enquiries: 08457 484950 or **www.nationalrail.com.uk**

Bus Travel
Peakland's towns and many of the villages are served by bus. Information is available from Traveline on 0871 200 22 33 or **www.traveline.info**

Weather
Online weather forecasts for the Peak District are available from the Met Office at **www.metoffice.gov.uk/loutdoor/mountainsafety/** and the Mountain Weather Information Service at **www.mwis.org.uk/**